45 Frying Recipes for Home

By: Kelly Johnson

Table of Contents

- Classic Fried Chicken with Buttermilk Marinade
- Crispy Beer-Battered Fish and Chips
- Tempura Shrimp with Soy Dipping Sauce
- Southern-Style Fried Catfish
- Zesty Fried Pickles with Ranch Dressing
- Onion Rings with a Light and Crispy Coating
- Homemade Chicken Tenders with Honey Mustard
- Fried Green Tomatoes with Remoulade Sauce
- Coconut Shrimp with Piña Colada Dipping Sauce
- Crispy Calamari Rings with Marinara
- Spicy Buffalo Cauliflower Bites
- Cornmeal-Fried Okra with Cajun Aioli
- Fried Mozzarella Sticks with Marinara
- Buttermilk Fried Pork Chops
- Garlic Parmesan Chicken Wings
- Sweet Potato Fries with Chipotle Mayo
- Japanese Tonkatsu with Tangy Bulldog Sauce
- Falafel Patties with Tahini Drizzle
- Southern Fried Chicken Livers
- Korean Fried Chicken with Gochujang Glaze
- Fried Mac and Cheese Bites
- Crispy Fried Tofu with Soy-Ginger Glaze
- Spanish Churros with Chocolate Dipping Sauce
- Indian Pakoras with Mint Chutney
- Potato Latkes with Applesauce
- Szechuan Orange Chicken
- Fried Ravioli with Marinara
- Homemade Corn Dogs with Mustard
- Buttermilk Fried Oysters with Lemon Aioli
- Coconut-Crusted Banana Fritters
- General Tso's Cauliflower
- Crab Rangoon with Sweet and Sour Sauce
- Fried Avocado Tacos with Lime Crema
- Jamaican Festival Dumplings
- Crispy Fried Egg Rolls with Sweet Chili Sauce

- Cajun Fried Turkey for a Festive Twist
- Cheddar Jalapeño Hush Puppies
- Italian Arancini Stuffed with Mozzarella
- Tempura Vegetables with Ponzu Sauce
- Beer-Battered Onion Petals
- Shrimp Po' Boy Sandwiches with Remoulade
- Fried Banana Spring Rolls with Caramel Sauce
- Greek Spanakopita Triangles
- Chicken Fried Steak with Country Gravy
- Fried Ice Cream Balls with Cinnamon Sugar

Classic Fried Chicken with Buttermilk Marinade

Ingredients:

- 3 pounds chicken pieces (legs, thighs, wings, and/or breasts)
- 2 cups buttermilk
- 2 cups all-purpose flour
- 1 tablespoon salt
- 1 tablespoon black pepper
- 1 teaspoon paprika
- 1 teaspoon garlic powder
- 1 teaspoon onion powder
- Vegetable oil for frying

Instructions:

Marinate the Chicken:
- Place the chicken pieces in a large bowl and pour buttermilk over them, ensuring each piece is well-coated.
- Cover the bowl and refrigerate for at least 4 hours or overnight, allowing the buttermilk to tenderize and flavor the chicken.

Prepare the Coating Mixture:
- In a shallow dish, mix the flour, salt, black pepper, paprika, garlic powder, and onion powder.

Coat the Chicken:
- Remove the chicken from the buttermilk, allowing excess to drip off.
- Dredge each piece in the seasoned flour mixture, pressing the flour onto the chicken to ensure a thick coating.

Heat the Oil:
- In a large, deep skillet or Dutch oven, heat about 2 inches of vegetable oil over medium-high heat until it reaches 350°F (180°C).

Fry the Chicken:
- Carefully place the coated chicken pieces in the hot oil, skin side down, without crowding the pan.
- Fry for about 12-15 minutes per side or until the internal temperature reaches 165°F (74°C) and the coating is golden brown and crispy.

Drain and Rest:

- Remove the fried chicken from the oil and place it on a wire rack or paper towels to drain any excess oil.
- Allow the chicken to rest for a few minutes before serving.

Serve:
- Serve the classic fried chicken hot, either on its own or with your favorite dipping sauces.

Enjoy the crispy and flavorful delight of classic fried chicken with a tenderized and buttermilk-infused twist!

Crispy Beer-Battered Fish and Chips

Ingredients:

For the Fish:

- 1 pound white fish fillets (cod, haddock, or similar)
- 1 cup all-purpose flour
- 1 cup cold beer (lager or ale)
- 1 teaspoon baking powder
- 1/2 teaspoon salt
- Vegetable oil for frying

For the Chips:

- 4 large potatoes, peeled and cut into thick strips
- Vegetable oil for deep-frying
- Salt to taste

Instructions:

Prepare the Fish:

Preheat the Oil:
- In a deep fryer or large, deep skillet, heat enough vegetable oil to submerge the fish pieces to 350°F (180°C).

Mix the Batter:
- In a bowl, whisk together the flour, cold beer, baking powder, and salt until you have a smooth batter. Let it rest for 15-20 minutes.

Coat the Fish:
- Pat the fish fillets dry with paper towels.
- Dip each fillet into the beer batter, ensuring it's well-coated.

Fry the Fish:
- Carefully place the beer-battered fish into the hot oil, a few pieces at a time, and fry until golden brown and crispy, about 4-6 minutes per side.

Drain and Keep Warm:
- Use a slotted spoon to transfer the fried fish to a plate lined with paper towels to drain any excess oil. Keep warm in a low oven while you prepare the chips.

Prepare the Chips:

- Preheat the Oil for Chips:
    - Heat additional vegetable oil in the fryer or a separate pot to 350°F (180°C).
- Fry the Chips:
    - Fry the potato strips in batches until golden brown and crispy, about 3-4 minutes per batch. Remove with a slotted spoon and drain on paper towels.
- Season the Chips:
    - Immediately sprinkle the hot chips with salt while they are still slightly oily.

Serve:

Serve the crispy beer-battered fish alongside the golden chips.
Optionally, serve with tartar sauce, malt vinegar, or your preferred dipping sauces.

Enjoy the classic combination of crispy beer-battered fish and golden, perfectly fried chips for a delightful and satisfying meal!

Tempura Shrimp with Soy Dipping Sauce

Ingredients:

For the Tempura Shrimp:

- 1 pound large shrimp, peeled and deveined
- 1 cup all-purpose flour
- 1 cup ice-cold sparkling water
- 1 egg, beaten
- Ice cubes
- Vegetable oil for frying
- Salt to taste

For the Soy Dipping Sauce:

- 1/4 cup soy sauce
- 1 tablespoon rice vinegar
- 1 teaspoon sugar
- 1/2 teaspoon grated ginger
- 1/2 teaspoon minced garlic
- 1 green onion, finely chopped (optional)

Instructions:

Prepare the Tempura Shrimp:

Preheat the Oil:
- In a deep fryer or large, deep skillet, heat vegetable oil to 350°F (180°C).

Prepare the Batter:
- In a mixing bowl, combine the flour, ice-cold sparkling water, beaten egg, and a handful of ice cubes. Mix gently until just combined; the batter should be lumpy.

Coat the Shrimp:
- Dip each shrimp into the tempura batter, ensuring it's fully coated.

Fry the Shrimp:

- Carefully place the coated shrimp into the hot oil, a few at a time, and fry until golden brown and crispy, about 2-3 minutes per side.

Drain and Season:
- Use a slotted spoon to transfer the tempura shrimp to a plate lined with paper towels to drain any excess oil. Sprinkle with salt while still hot.

Prepare the Soy Dipping Sauce:

Mix Ingredients:
- In a small bowl, combine soy sauce, rice vinegar, sugar, grated ginger, minced garlic, and chopped green onion (if using). Stir until the sugar dissolves.

Serve:
- Serve the tempura shrimp hot with the soy dipping sauce on the side.

Tips:

- Tempura is best served immediately for optimal crispiness.
- You can also try serving with a squeeze of lemon or lime for added freshness.

Enjoy these light and crispy tempura shrimp with a flavorful soy dipping sauce for a delightful appetizer or main course!

Southern-Style Fried Catfish

Ingredients:

- 4 catfish fillets
- 1 cup buttermilk
- 1 cup cornmeal
- 1 cup all-purpose flour
- 1 teaspoon salt
- 1 teaspoon black pepper
- 1/2 teaspoon cayenne pepper (optional for heat)
- Vegetable oil for frying

Instructions:

Marinate the Catfish:
- Place catfish fillets in a dish and pour buttermilk over them. Let them marinate for at least 30 minutes to an hour in the refrigerator.

Prepare the Coating:
- In a shallow dish, mix cornmeal, flour, salt, black pepper, and cayenne pepper (if using).

Coat the Catfish:
- Remove catfish from the buttermilk, letting excess liquid drip off.
- Dredge each fillet in the cornmeal mixture, ensuring an even coating.

Heat the Oil:
- In a large, deep skillet or Dutch oven, heat about 2 inches of vegetable oil to 350°F (180°C).

Fry the Catfish:
- Carefully place the coated catfish fillets into the hot oil, a few at a time, and fry until golden brown and crispy, about 4-5 minutes per side.

Drain and Rest:
- Use a slotted spoon to transfer the fried catfish to a plate lined with paper towels to drain any excess oil.
- Allow the catfish to rest for a few minutes before serving.

Serve:
- Serve the Southern-style fried catfish hot, with your favorite side dishes and dipping sauces.

Tips:

- For an extra touch of Southern flavor, serve with hushpuppies, coleslaw, or a squeeze of lemon.
- Adjust the cayenne pepper to your preferred level of spiciness.

Enjoy the classic Southern comfort of crispy and flavorful fried catfish!

Zesty Fried Pickles with Ranch Dressing

Ingredients:

For the Fried Pickles:

- 1 cup dill pickle slices, drained
- 1 cup buttermilk
- 1 cup all-purpose flour
- 1 teaspoon garlic powder
- 1 teaspoon paprika
- 1/2 teaspoon cayenne pepper (adjust to taste)
- Vegetable oil for frying

For the Ranch Dressing:

- 1/2 cup mayonnaise
- 1/2 cup sour cream
- 1 tablespoon chopped fresh parsley
- 1 tablespoon chopped fresh chives
- 1 teaspoon dried dill
- 1 teaspoon garlic powder
- Salt and black pepper to taste

Instructions:

Prepare the Fried Pickles:

Marinate the Pickles:
- Place pickle slices in a bowl and pour buttermilk over them. Let them marinate for at least 30 minutes to an hour in the refrigerator.

Prepare the Coating:
- In a shallow dish, mix flour, garlic powder, paprika, and cayenne pepper.

Coat the Pickles:
- Remove pickles from the buttermilk, letting excess liquid drip off.
- Dredge each pickle slice in the flour mixture, ensuring an even coating.

Heat the Oil:

- In a deep fryer or large, deep skillet, heat vegetable oil to 375°F (190°C).

Fry the Pickles:
- Carefully place the coated pickle slices into the hot oil, a few at a time, and fry until golden brown and crispy, about 1-2 minutes per side.

Drain:
- Use a slotted spoon to transfer the fried pickles to a plate lined with paper towels to drain any excess oil.

Prepare the Ranch Dressing:

Mix Ingredients:
- In a small bowl, combine mayonnaise, sour cream, parsley, chives, dried dill, garlic powder, salt, and black pepper. Mix until well combined.

Serve:
- Serve the zesty fried pickles hot with a side of homemade ranch dressing for dipping.

Tips:

- Experiment with different pickle varieties, such as bread and butter pickles or spicy pickles, for a unique twist.
- Adjust the level of cayenne pepper in the coating to suit your desired spiciness.

Enjoy the zesty kick of these crispy fried pickles paired with a cool and creamy ranch dressing!

Onion Rings with a Light and Crispy Coating

Ingredients:

- 2 large onions, cut into rings
- 1 cup buttermilk
- 1 cup all-purpose flour
- 1 teaspoon garlic powder
- 1 teaspoon smoked paprika
- 1/2 teaspoon cayenne pepper (adjust to taste)
- Salt and black pepper to taste
- Vegetable oil for frying

Instructions:

Soak the Onions:
- Separate the onion rings and place them in a bowl. Pour buttermilk over the onions, ensuring they are well-coated. Let them soak for at least 30 minutes to an hour in the refrigerator.

Prepare the Coating:
- In a shallow dish, mix flour, garlic powder, smoked paprika, cayenne pepper, salt, and black pepper.

Coat the Onion Rings:
- Remove onion rings from the buttermilk, letting excess liquid drip off.
- Dredge each onion ring in the flour mixture, ensuring an even coating.

Heat the Oil:
- In a deep fryer or large, deep skillet, heat vegetable oil to 375°F (190°C).

Fry the Onion Rings:
- Carefully place the coated onion rings into the hot oil, a few at a time, and fry until golden brown and crispy, about 2-3 minutes per side.

Drain:
- Use a slotted spoon to transfer the fried onion rings to a plate lined with paper towels to drain any excess oil.

Serve:
- Serve the onion rings hot as a delightful appetizer or side dish.

Tips:

- For an extra crunch, you can double-coat the onion rings by dipping them back into the buttermilk and flour mixture.
- Experiment with different seasonings in the coating, such as onion powder or your favorite herbs.

Enjoy these light and crispy onion rings with their flavorful coating for a delicious and satisfying snack or side dish!

Homemade Chicken Tenders with Honey Mustard

Ingredients:

For the Chicken Tenders:

- 1 pound chicken tenders
- 1 cup buttermilk
- 1 cup all-purpose flour
- 1 teaspoon garlic powder
- 1 teaspoon onion powder
- 1/2 teaspoon paprika
- Salt and black pepper to taste
- Vegetable oil for frying

For the Honey Mustard Sauce:

- 1/2 cup mayonnaise
- 2 tablespoons Dijon mustard
- 2 tablespoons honey
- 1 teaspoon lemon juice
- Salt and black pepper to taste

Instructions:

Prepare the Chicken Tenders:

Marinate the Chicken:
- Place chicken tenders in a bowl and pour buttermilk over them. Let them marinate for at least 30 minutes to an hour in the refrigerator.

Prepare the Coating:
- In a shallow dish, mix flour, garlic powder, onion powder, paprika, salt, and black pepper.

Coat the Chicken:
- Remove chicken tenders from the buttermilk, letting excess liquid drip off.
- Dredge each chicken tender in the flour mixture, ensuring an even coating.

Heat the Oil:

- In a deep fryer or large, deep skillet, heat vegetable oil to 375°F (190°C).

Fry the Chicken Tenders:
- Carefully place the coated chicken tenders into the hot oil, a few at a time, and fry until golden brown and cooked through, about 3-4 minutes per side.

Drain:
- Use a slotted spoon to transfer the fried chicken tenders to a plate lined with paper towels to drain any excess oil.

Prepare the Honey Mustard Sauce:

Mix Ingredients:
- In a small bowl, combine mayonnaise, Dijon mustard, honey, lemon juice, salt, and black pepper. Mix until well combined.

Serve:
- Serve the homemade chicken tenders hot with a side of delicious honey mustard sauce for dipping.

Tips:

- Adjust the seasonings in the flour mixture to suit your taste preferences.
- For a lighter version, you can bake the coated chicken tenders in the oven at 400°F (200°C) until golden brown and cooked through.

Enjoy these crispy and flavorful homemade chicken tenders with a sweet and tangy honey mustard sauce!

Fried Green Tomatoes with Remoulade Sauce

Ingredients:

For the Fried Green Tomatoes:

- 4 large green tomatoes, sliced into 1/4-inch rounds
- 1 cup buttermilk
- 1 cup cornmeal
- 1/2 cup all-purpose flour
- 1 teaspoon garlic powder
- 1 teaspoon onion powder
- 1/2 teaspoon paprika
- Salt and black pepper to taste
- Vegetable oil for frying

For the Remoulade Sauce:

- 1/2 cup mayonnaise
- 2 tablespoons Dijon mustard
- 1 tablespoon chopped capers
- 1 tablespoon chopped dill pickles
- 1 tablespoon chopped fresh parsley
- 1 teaspoon hot sauce
- 1 teaspoon Worcestershire sauce
- 1 clove garlic, minced
- Salt and black pepper to taste

Instructions:

Prepare the Fried Green Tomatoes:

Soak the Tomatoes:
- Place tomato slices in a bowl and pour buttermilk over them. Let them soak for at least 30 minutes in the refrigerator.

Prepare the Coating:
- In a shallow dish, mix cornmeal, flour, garlic powder, onion powder, paprika, salt, and black pepper.

Coat the Tomatoes:
- Remove tomato slices from the buttermilk, letting excess liquid drip off.

- Dredge each tomato slice in the cornmeal mixture, ensuring an even coating.

Heat the Oil:
- In a deep fryer or large, deep skillet, heat vegetable oil to 375°F (190°C).

Fry the Green Tomatoes:
- Carefully place the coated tomato slices into the hot oil, a few at a time, and fry until golden brown and crispy, about 2-3 minutes per side.

Drain:
- Use a slotted spoon to transfer the fried green tomatoes to a plate lined with paper towels to drain any excess oil.

Prepare the Remoulade Sauce:

Mix Ingredients:
- In a small bowl, combine mayonnaise, Dijon mustard, capers, dill pickles, parsley, hot sauce, Worcestershire sauce, minced garlic, salt, and black pepper. Mix until well combined.

Serve:
- Serve the fried green tomatoes hot with a side of zesty remoulade sauce for dipping.

Tips:

- Experiment with adding a pinch of cayenne pepper or Creole seasoning to the remoulade sauce for extra flavor.
- Serve the fried green tomatoes as an appetizer, side dish, or even as a unique topping for burgers or sandwiches.

Enjoy the crispy and tangy goodness of fried green tomatoes with a flavorful remoulade sauce!

Coconut Shrimp with Piña Colada Dipping Sauce

Ingredients:

For the Coconut Shrimp:

- 1 pound large shrimp, peeled and deveined
- 1 cup all-purpose flour
- 3 large eggs, beaten
- 2 cups sweetened shredded coconut
- 1 cup Panko breadcrumbs
- Salt and black pepper to taste
- Vegetable oil for frying

For the Piña Colada Dipping Sauce:

- 1 cup pineapple juice
- 1/2 cup coconut cream
- 1/4 cup Greek yogurt
- 2 tablespoons honey
- 1 tablespoon lime juice
- 1 teaspoon rum extract (optional)
- Pinch of salt

Instructions:

Prepare the Coconut Shrimp:

Prepare the Breading Station:
- Set up a breading station with three shallow dishes - one with flour, one with beaten eggs, and one with a mixture of shredded coconut and Panko breadcrumbs.

Coat the Shrimp:
- Season shrimp with salt and black pepper.
- Dredge each shrimp in the flour, dip into the beaten eggs, and then coat with the coconut-Panko mixture, pressing gently to adhere.

Chill the Shrimp:

- Place the coated shrimp on a baking sheet and refrigerate for at least 30 minutes to help the coating adhere.

Heat the Oil:
- In a deep fryer or large, deep skillet, heat vegetable oil to 350°F (175°C).

Fry the Coconut Shrimp:
- Carefully place the coated shrimp into the hot oil, a few at a time, and fry until golden brown and crispy, about 2-3 minutes per side.

Drain:
- Use a slotted spoon to transfer the fried coconut shrimp to a plate lined with paper towels to drain any excess oil.

Prepare the Piña Colada Dipping Sauce:

Mix Ingredients:
- In a small bowl, whisk together pineapple juice, coconut cream, Greek yogurt, honey, lime juice, rum extract (if using), and a pinch of salt.

Chill:
- Refrigerate the dipping sauce until ready to serve.

Serve:

- Serve the crispy coconut shrimp hot with the refreshing piña colada dipping sauce on the side.

Tips:

- For an extra tropical touch, you can add a splash of rum to the piña colada dipping sauce.
- Ensure the oil is at the right temperature for frying to achieve a golden and crispy coating on the shrimp.

Enjoy these delightful coconut shrimp with a piña colada dipping sauce for a taste of the tropics!

Crispy Calamari Rings with Marinara

Ingredients:

For the Calamari Rings:

- 1 pound fresh calamari, cleaned and sliced into rings
- 1 cup buttermilk
- 1 cup all-purpose flour
- 1 teaspoon garlic powder
- 1 teaspoon onion powder
- 1/2 teaspoon paprika
- Salt and black pepper to taste
- Vegetable oil for frying

For the Marinara Sauce:

- 1 can (28 ounces) crushed tomatoes
- 2 cloves garlic, minced
- 1 teaspoon dried oregano
- 1 teaspoon dried basil
- 1/2 teaspoon red pepper flakes (optional)
- Salt and black pepper to taste
- 2 tablespoons olive oil

Instructions:

Prepare the Calamari Rings:

   Soak the Calamari:
   - Place calamari rings in a bowl and pour buttermilk over them. Let them soak for at least 30 minutes in the refrigerator.

   Prepare the Coating:
   - In a shallow dish, mix flour, garlic powder, onion powder, paprika, salt, and black pepper.

   Coat the Calamari:
   - Remove calamari rings from the buttermilk, letting excess liquid drip off.

- Dredge each calamari ring in the flour mixture, ensuring an even coating.

Heat the Oil:
- In a deep fryer or large, deep skillet, heat vegetable oil to 375°F (190°C).

Fry the Calamari Rings:
- Carefully place the coated calamari rings into the hot oil, a few at a time, and fry until golden brown and crispy, about 2 minutes per side.

Drain:
- Use a slotted spoon to transfer the fried calamari rings to a plate lined with paper towels to drain any excess oil.

Prepare the Marinara Sauce:

Sauté Garlic:
- In a saucepan, heat olive oil over medium heat. Add minced garlic and sauté until fragrant.

Add Tomatoes and Seasonings:
- Pour in crushed tomatoes and add oregano, basil, red pepper flakes (if using), salt, and black pepper. Stir to combine.

Simmer:
- Allow the marinara sauce to simmer for about 15-20 minutes, stirring occasionally, until it thickens.

Serve:

- Serve the crispy calamari rings hot with a side of marinara sauce for dipping.

Tips:

- Add a squeeze of lemon over the fried calamari rings for a burst of freshness.
- Experiment with different seasonings in the flour mixture, such as cayenne pepper or Italian herbs.

Enjoy these crispy calamari rings with a flavorful marinara sauce for a delicious appetizer or snack!

Spicy Buffalo Cauliflower Bites

Ingredients:

For the Buffalo Cauliflower Bites:

- 1 large head of cauliflower, cut into florets
- 1 cup all-purpose flour
- 1 cup water
- 1 teaspoon garlic powder
- 1 teaspoon onion powder
- 1/2 teaspoon smoked paprika
- Salt and black pepper to taste
- Cooking spray

For the Buffalo Sauce:

- 1/2 cup hot sauce (such as Frank's RedHot)
- 1/4 cup unsalted butter, melted
- 1 tablespoon honey (optional, for sweetness)
- 1 teaspoon garlic powder
- 1 teaspoon onion powder

Instructions:

Prepare the Buffalo Cauliflower Bites:

    Preheat the Oven:
- Preheat the oven to 450°F (230°C). Line a baking sheet with parchment paper.

    Make the Batter:
- In a large bowl, whisk together flour, water, garlic powder, onion powder, smoked paprika, salt, and black pepper until you have a smooth batter.

    Coat the Cauliflower:
- Dip each cauliflower floret into the batter, ensuring it is well coated. Shake off any excess batter.

    Arrange on Baking Sheet:

- Place the coated cauliflower florets on the prepared baking sheet, leaving space between each piece.

Bake:
- Bake in the preheated oven for 20-25 minutes or until the cauliflower is golden brown and crispy, flipping halfway through.

Prepare the Buffalo Sauce:
- While the cauliflower is baking, mix hot sauce, melted butter, honey (if using), garlic powder, and onion powder in a bowl.

Toss in Buffalo Sauce:
- Once the cauliflower is done, transfer it to a large bowl. Pour the buffalo sauce over the cauliflower and toss until evenly coated.

Bake Again:
- Place the coated cauliflower back on the baking sheet and bake for an additional 10 minutes or until the sauce is sticky and caramelized.

Serve:

- Serve the spicy buffalo cauliflower bites hot with your favorite dipping sauce.

Tips:

- Adjust the level of spiciness by adding more or less hot sauce to the buffalo sauce mixture.
- Serve with a side of ranch or blue cheese dressing for dipping.

Enjoy these spicy buffalo cauliflower bites as a flavorful and vegetarian-friendly alternative to traditional buffalo wings!

Cornmeal-Fried Okra with Cajun Aioli

Ingredients:

For the Cornmeal-Fried Okra:

- 1 pound fresh okra, sliced into 1/2-inch rounds
- 1 cup cornmeal
- 1/2 cup all-purpose flour
- 1 teaspoon garlic powder
- 1 teaspoon onion powder
- 1/2 teaspoon smoked paprika
- Salt and black pepper to taste
- 1 cup buttermilk
- Vegetable oil for frying

For the Cajun Aioli:

- 1/2 cup mayonnaise
- 1 tablespoon Dijon mustard
- 1 teaspoon Cajun seasoning
- 1 clove garlic, minced
- 1 tablespoon fresh lemon juice
- Salt and black pepper to taste

Instructions:

Prepare the Cajun Aioli:

   Mix Ingredients:
   - In a small bowl, whisk together mayonnaise, Dijon mustard, Cajun seasoning, minced garlic, fresh lemon juice, salt, and black pepper. Adjust the seasoning to taste.

   Chill:
   - Cover the Cajun aioli and refrigerate while preparing the cornmeal-fried okra.

Prepare the Cornmeal-Fried Okra:

- Preheat the Oil:
  - In a large, deep skillet, heat vegetable oil to 350°F (175°C).
- Prepare the Batter:
  - In a shallow dish, combine cornmeal, flour, garlic powder, onion powder, smoked paprika, salt, and black pepper.
- Dip in Buttermilk:
  - Dip each okra round into the buttermilk, allowing any excess to drip off.
- Coat in Cornmeal Mixture:
  - Coat the okra in the cornmeal mixture, pressing gently to adhere the coating.
- Fry the Okra:
  - Carefully place the coated okra rounds into the hot oil, a few at a time, and fry until golden brown and crispy, about 2-3 minutes per side.
- Drain:
  - Use a slotted spoon to transfer the fried okra to a plate lined with paper towels to drain any excess oil.

Serve:

- Serve the cornmeal-fried okra hot with the Cajun aioli on the side for dipping.

Tips:

- Adjust the Cajun seasoning in the aioli according to your preferred level of spiciness.
- For extra crunch, you can double-coat the okra by dipping it back into the buttermilk and cornmeal mixture before frying.

Enjoy these cornmeal-fried okra rounds with a flavorful Cajun aioli for a delicious and crispy appetizer or side dish!

Fried Mozzarella Sticks with Marinara

Ingredients:

For the Fried Mozzarella Sticks:

- 8 ounces mozzarella cheese, cut into sticks
- 1 cup breadcrumbs
- 1/2 cup all-purpose flour
- 2 large eggs, beaten
- 1 teaspoon dried oregano
- 1 teaspoon dried basil
- 1/2 teaspoon garlic powder
- Salt and black pepper to taste
- Vegetable oil for frying

For the Marinara Sauce:

- 1 can (14 ounces) crushed tomatoes
- 1 clove garlic, minced
- 1 teaspoon dried oregano
- 1 teaspoon dried basil
- 1/2 teaspoon sugar
- Salt and black pepper to taste
- 2 tablespoons olive oil

Instructions:

Prepare the Marinara Sauce:

Sauté Garlic:
- In a saucepan, heat olive oil over medium heat. Add minced garlic and sauté until fragrant.

Add Tomatoes and Seasonings:
- Pour in crushed tomatoes and add oregano, basil, sugar, salt, and black pepper. Stir to combine.

Simmer:
- Allow the marinara sauce to simmer for about 15-20 minutes, stirring occasionally, until it thickens.

Prepare the Fried Mozzarella Sticks:

Preheat the Oil:
- In a deep fryer or large, deep skillet, heat vegetable oil to 350°F (175°C).

Prepare the Breading Station:
- In one shallow dish, place flour. In another, mix breadcrumbs, dried oregano, dried basil, garlic powder, salt, and black pepper. In a third dish, beat the eggs.

Coat the Mozzarella Sticks:
- Dip each mozzarella stick into the flour, then into the beaten eggs, and finally into the breadcrumb mixture, ensuring an even coating.

Double Coat (Optional):
- For an extra crispy texture, you can repeat the process, dipping the mozzarella sticks back into the beaten eggs and breadcrumbs.

Fry the Mozzarella Sticks:
- Carefully place the coated mozzarella sticks into the hot oil, a few at a time, and fry until golden brown, about 2-3 minutes.

Drain:
- Use a slotted spoon to transfer the fried mozzarella sticks to a plate lined with paper towels to drain any excess oil.

Serve:

- Serve the hot fried mozzarella sticks with the marinara sauce for dipping.

Tips:

- Make sure the oil is at the correct temperature to achieve a crispy exterior while keeping the cheese inside melted.
- Freeze the coated mozzarella sticks for about 30 minutes before frying for a firmer texture.

Enjoy these homemade fried mozzarella sticks with a flavorful marinara sauce as a crowd-pleasing appetizer or snack!

Buttermilk Fried Pork Chops

Ingredients:

- 4 bone-in pork chops
- 2 cups buttermilk
- 2 cups all-purpose flour
- 1 teaspoon garlic powder
- 1 teaspoon onion powder
- 1 teaspoon paprika
- Salt and black pepper to taste
- Vegetable oil for frying

Instructions:

Marinate the Pork Chops:
- Place the pork chops in a shallow dish and pour buttermilk over them. Ensure the chops are fully coated. Marinate in the refrigerator for at least 4 hours or overnight.

Prepare the Breading Mixture:
- In a separate bowl, combine flour, garlic powder, onion powder, paprika, salt, and black pepper. Mix well to create the breading mixture.

Bread the Pork Chops:
- Remove the marinated pork chops from the buttermilk, allowing any excess to drip off. Coat each chop in the breading mixture, pressing the flour mixture onto the chops to ensure a good coating.

Rest the Breaded Chops:
- Place the breaded pork chops on a wire rack and let them rest for about 15-20 minutes. This helps the coating adhere better during frying.

Preheat the Oil:
- In a large skillet or deep fryer, heat vegetable oil to 350°F (175°C).

Fry the Pork Chops:
- Carefully place the breaded pork chops into the hot oil, working in batches if necessary. Fry until golden brown on both sides, approximately 5-7 minutes per side or until the internal temperature reaches 145°F (63°C).

Drain and Rest:

- Use tongs to transfer the fried pork chops to a plate lined with paper towels to drain any excess oil. Let them rest for a few minutes before serving.

Serve:
- Serve the buttermilk-fried pork chops hot, garnished with fresh herbs if desired.

Tips:

- For extra flavor, you can add additional seasonings like cayenne pepper or smoked paprika to the breading mixture.
- Ensure the oil is at the correct temperature to achieve a crispy and golden exterior on the pork chops.

Enjoy these buttermilk-fried pork chops for a delicious and comforting meal!

Garlic Parmesan Chicken Wings

Ingredients:

For the Chicken Wings:

- 2 pounds chicken wings, split at joints, tips discarded
- 1 cup all-purpose flour
- 1 teaspoon garlic powder
- 1 teaspoon onion powder
- Salt and black pepper to taste
- Vegetable oil for frying

For the Garlic Parmesan Sauce:

- 1/2 cup unsalted butter
- 4 cloves garlic, minced
- 1/2 cup grated Parmesan cheese
- 1 teaspoon dried parsley flakes
- Salt and black pepper to taste

Instructions:

Prepare the Chicken Wings:

    Coat the Wings:
- In a bowl, combine flour, garlic powder, onion powder, salt, and black pepper. Coat each chicken wing in the seasoned flour mixture, shaking off any excess.

    Rest the Wings:
- Place the coated wings on a wire rack and let them rest for about 15-20 minutes. This helps the coating adhere better during frying.

    Preheat the Oil:
- In a deep fryer or large skillet, heat vegetable oil to 375°F (190°C).

    Fry the Wings:
- Carefully place the coated wings into the hot oil, working in batches if necessary. Fry until golden brown and crispy, approximately 10-12 minutes. Ensure the internal temperature reaches at least 165°F (74°C).

    Drain and Rest:

- Use a slotted spoon to transfer the fried wings to a plate lined with paper towels to drain any excess oil.

Prepare the Garlic Parmesan Sauce:

Melt Butter:
- In a saucepan, melt the butter over medium heat.

Add Garlic:
- Add minced garlic to the melted butter and sauté until fragrant, about 1-2 minutes.

Combine Parmesan and Herbs:
- Stir in grated Parmesan cheese and dried parsley flakes. Season with salt and black pepper to taste.

Toss the Wings:
- Toss the fried wings in the garlic Parmesan sauce, ensuring they are well-coated.

Serve:

- Serve the garlic Parmesan chicken wings hot, garnished with additional Parmesan and chopped fresh parsley if desired.

Tips:

- Adjust the amount of garlic and Parmesan according to your taste preference.
- For a spicier version, you can add a pinch of cayenne pepper or red pepper flakes to the garlic Parmesan sauce.

Enjoy these crispy and flavorful garlic Parmesan chicken wings as a tasty appetizer or party snack!

Sweet Potato Fries with Chipotle Mayo

Ingredients:

For the Sweet Potato Fries:

- 2 large sweet potatoes, peeled and cut into matchsticks
- 2 tablespoons cornstarch
- 2 tablespoons olive oil
- 1 teaspoon paprika
- 1 teaspoon garlic powder
- 1/2 teaspoon cayenne pepper (optional)
- Salt and black pepper to taste

For the Chipotle Mayo:

- 1/2 cup mayonnaise
- 1-2 teaspoons adobo sauce from canned chipotle peppers
- 1 teaspoon lime juice
- Salt to taste

Instructions:

Prepare the Sweet Potato Fries:

Preheat the Oven:
- Preheat the oven to 425°F (220°C).

Coat the Fries:
- In a large bowl, toss the sweet potato matchsticks with cornstarch, olive oil, paprika, garlic powder, cayenne pepper (if using), salt, and black pepper until evenly coated.

Arrange on Baking Sheet:
- Spread the coated sweet potato fries in a single layer on a baking sheet lined with parchment paper, ensuring they are not crowded to allow for even baking.

Bake:

- Bake in the preheated oven for 20-25 minutes, flipping the fries halfway through, or until they are crispy and golden brown.

Prepare the Chipotle Mayo:

Mix Ingredients:
- In a small bowl, whisk together mayonnaise, adobo sauce, lime juice, and salt to taste. Adjust the level of spiciness by adding more or less adobo sauce.

Serve:

- Serve the hot sweet potato fries with the chipotle mayo on the side for dipping.

Tips:

- Adjust the seasoning of the sweet potato fries according to your taste preference.
- For an extra kick, sprinkle additional cayenne pepper or smoked paprika on the fries before baking.

Enjoy these crispy sweet potato fries with a smoky and spicy chipotle mayo dip for a delightful snack or side dish!

Japanese Tonkatsu with Tangy Bulldog Sauce

Ingredients:

For the Tonkatsu:

- 4 pork loin chops, boneless
- Salt and black pepper to taste
- 1 cup all-purpose flour
- 2 large eggs, beaten
- 2 cups panko breadcrumbs
- Vegetable oil for frying

For the Bulldog Sauce:

- 1/2 cup ketchup
- 2 tablespoons Worcestershire sauce
- 1 tablespoon soy sauce
- 1 tablespoon Dijon mustard
- 1 tablespoon sugar

Instructions:

Prepare the Tonkatsu:

Preheat the Oil:
- In a deep fryer or large skillet, heat vegetable oil to 350°F (175°C).

Season the Pork Chops:
- Season the pork loin chops with salt and black pepper.

Coat in Flour, Egg, and Panko:
- Dredge each pork chop in flour, then dip into beaten eggs, and coat with panko breadcrumbs, pressing the breadcrumbs onto the meat to adhere.

Fry the Tonkatsu:
- Carefully place the breaded pork chops into the hot oil, working in batches if necessary. Fry until golden brown and the internal temperature reaches 145°F (63°C), approximately 5-7 minutes per side.

Drain and Rest:
- Use a slotted spoon to transfer the fried tonkatsu to a plate lined with paper towels to drain any excess oil. Let them rest for a few minutes.

Prepare the Bulldog Sauce:

- Combine Ingredients:
  - In a small saucepan, combine ketchup, Worcestershire sauce, soy sauce, Dijon mustard, and sugar. Bring to a simmer over medium heat, stirring continuously.
- Simmer:
  - Reduce the heat and let the sauce simmer for 5-7 minutes or until it thickens slightly.

Serve:

- Serve the crispy tonkatsu hot, accompanied by the tangy Bulldog sauce for dipping.

Tips:

- Bulldog sauce is a popular Japanese condiment available in most Asian grocery stores. If unavailable, you can substitute it with a homemade version or your favorite tonkatsu sauce.
- Serve tonkatsu with shredded cabbage for an authentic touch.

Enjoy this classic Japanese tonkatsu with a flavorful and tangy Bulldog sauce for a satisfying meal!

Falafel Patties with Tahini Drizzle

Ingredients:

For the Falafel Patties:

- 2 cups cooked chickpeas, drained and rinsed
- 1 small onion, finely chopped
- 3 cloves garlic, minced
- 1/4 cup fresh parsley, chopped
- 1 teaspoon ground cumin
- 1 teaspoon ground coriander
- 1/2 teaspoon baking soda
- Salt and black pepper to taste
- 3 tablespoons all-purpose flour
- Vegetable oil for frying

For the Tahini Drizzle:

- 1/2 cup tahini
- 2 tablespoons lemon juice
- 2 tablespoons water
- 2 tablespoons olive oil
- 1 clove garlic, minced
- Salt to taste

Instructions:

Prepare the Falafel Patties:

Combine Ingredients:
- In a food processor, combine chickpeas, onion, garlic, parsley, cumin, coriander, baking soda, salt, and black pepper. Process until the mixture becomes a coarse paste.

Add Flour:
- Transfer the mixture to a bowl and stir in the all-purpose flour. Mix until well combined.

Shape Patties:
- With wet hands, shape the mixture into small patties, about 1.5 inches in diameter.

Fry the Falafel:
- In a skillet, heat vegetable oil over medium heat. Fry the falafel patties until golden brown and crispy, about 3-4 minutes per side. Transfer to a plate lined with paper towels to drain excess oil.

Prepare the Tahini Drizzle:

Whisk Ingredients:
- In a bowl, whisk together tahini, lemon juice, water, olive oil, minced garlic, and salt. Adjust the consistency by adding more water if needed.

Serve:

- Serve the falafel patties hot, drizzled with the tahini sauce.

Tips:

- You can also bake the falafel patties in a preheated oven at 375°F (190°C) for about 20-25 minutes, flipping halfway through.
- Serve falafel with pita bread, salad, and additional tahini drizzle for a complete meal.

Enjoy these flavorful falafel patties with a creamy tahini drizzle for a delicious and satisfying dish!

Southern Fried Chicken Livers

Ingredients:

- 1 pound chicken livers, cleaned and trimmed
- 1 cup buttermilk
- 1 cup all-purpose flour
- 1 teaspoon garlic powder
- 1 teaspoon onion powder
- 1/2 teaspoon paprika
- Salt and black pepper to taste
- Vegetable oil for frying

Instructions:

Soak in Buttermilk:
- Place the cleaned chicken livers in a bowl and cover them with buttermilk. Let them soak for at least 30 minutes to an hour.

Prepare Coating Mixture:
- In a separate bowl, combine flour, garlic powder, onion powder, paprika, salt, and black pepper. Mix well to create the coating mixture.

Coat Livers:
- Remove the chicken livers from the buttermilk, allowing any excess liquid to drip off. Dredge each liver in the flour mixture, ensuring they are evenly coated.

Heat Oil:
- In a skillet or deep fryer, heat vegetable oil to 350°F (175°C).

Fry the Livers:
- Carefully place the coated chicken livers into the hot oil. Fry for 3-4 minutes per side or until they are golden brown and cooked through.

Drain and Serve:
- Use a slotted spoon to transfer the fried chicken livers to a plate lined with paper towels to drain any excess oil.

Serve Warm:
- Serve the Southern fried chicken livers warm as a snack or side dish.

Tips:

- Adjust the seasoning in the flour mixture according to your taste preference.
- Serve with your favorite dipping sauce or hot sauce for added flavor.

Enjoy these Southern fried chicken livers as a flavorful and crispy delicacy

Korean Fried Chicken with Gochujang Glaze

Ingredients:

For the Chicken:

- 2 pounds chicken wings or drumettes
- Salt and pepper to taste
- 1 cup buttermilk
- 1 cup all-purpose flour
- Vegetable oil for frying

For the Gochujang Glaze:

- 1/4 cup gochujang (Korean red pepper paste)
- 3 tablespoons soy sauce
- 2 tablespoons honey
- 1 tablespoon rice vinegar
- 1 tablespoon sesame oil
- 2 cloves garlic, minced
- 1 teaspoon grated ginger
- Sesame seeds and chopped green onions for garnish

Instructions:

Prepare the Chicken:

  Season and Soak:
  - Season the chicken with salt and pepper. Place the chicken in a bowl, pour buttermilk over it, and let it soak for at least 1 hour or overnight in the refrigerator.

  Coat in Flour:
  - Remove the chicken from the buttermilk, allowing excess to drip off. Dredge each piece in flour, ensuring an even coating.

  Fry the Chicken:
  - In a large skillet or deep fryer, heat vegetable oil to 350°F (175°C). Fry the chicken in batches until golden brown and cooked through, about 8-10 minutes. Transfer to a plate lined with paper towels.

Prepare the Gochujang Glaze:

Combine Ingredients:
- In a bowl, whisk together gochujang, soy sauce, honey, rice vinegar, sesame oil, minced garlic, and grated ginger.

Heat and Glaze:
- Heat the glaze in a saucepan over medium heat until it thickens slightly. Toss the fried chicken in the glaze until evenly coated.

Garnish and Serve:
- Transfer the glazed chicken to a serving platter, and garnish with sesame seeds and chopped green onions.

Tips:

- Adjust the spice level by adding more or less gochujang according to your preference.
- Serve the Korean fried chicken with pickled radishes or kimchi for an authentic experience.

Enjoy this Korean Fried Chicken with Gochujang Glaze for a flavorful and crispy treat!

Fried Mac and Cheese Bites

Ingredients:

- 2 cups cooked macaroni and cheese, chilled and firm
- 1 cup all-purpose flour
- 2 large eggs, beaten
- 1 cup breadcrumbs
- Vegetable oil for frying
- Marinara sauce for dipping (optional)

Instructions:

Prepare Mac and Cheese:
- Cook your favorite macaroni and cheese according to the package instructions. Allow it to chill and firm up in the refrigerator for at least 2 hours or overnight.

Shape into Bites:
- Once the mac and cheese is firm, use your hands or a cookie scoop to shape it into bite-sized balls.

Coat in Flour, Eggs, and Breadcrumbs:
- Set up a breading station with three bowls: one with flour, one with beaten eggs, and one with breadcrumbs. Roll each mac and cheese bite in the flour, dip it in the beaten eggs, and coat it with breadcrumbs, ensuring an even coating.

Chill Again (Optional):
- For an extra crispy texture, place the coated mac and cheese bites back in the refrigerator for about 30 minutes.

Heat Oil:
- In a deep fryer or large skillet, heat vegetable oil to 350°F (175°C).

Fry the Bites:
- Carefully place the coated mac and cheese bites into the hot oil in batches. Fry until they are golden brown and crispy, about 2-3 minutes. Use a slotted spoon to transfer them to a plate lined with paper towels.

Serve and Dip:
- Serve the fried mac and cheese bites hot with marinara sauce for dipping if desired.

Tips:

- Experiment with different types of cheese or add-ins for your mac and cheese for unique flavors.
- Make sure the oil is hot enough to achieve a crispy exterior.

Enjoy these Fried Mac and Cheese Bites as a delightful appetizer or snack!

Crispy Fried Tofu with Soy-Ginger Glaze

Ingredients:

For the Crispy Fried Tofu:

- 1 block firm or extra-firm tofu, pressed and cut into cubes
- 1 cup cornstarch
- Vegetable oil for frying
- Salt to taste

For the Soy-Ginger Glaze:

- 1/4 cup soy sauce
- 2 tablespoons rice vinegar
- 2 tablespoons maple syrup or agave nectar
- 1 tablespoon sesame oil
- 1 tablespoon grated ginger
- 2 cloves garlic, minced
- 1 tablespoon cornstarch mixed with 2 tablespoons water (cornstarch slurry)

Instructions:

Crispy Fried Tofu:

Press Tofu:
- Press the tofu to remove excess moisture. Cut it into bite-sized cubes.

Coat in Cornstarch:
- Roll each tofu cube in cornstarch until well coated.

Heat Oil:
- In a large skillet or wok, heat vegetable oil over medium-high heat.

Fry Tofu:
- Fry the coated tofu cubes in batches until they are golden brown and crispy on all sides. Remove and place on a plate lined with paper towels to drain excess oil. Sprinkle with salt to taste.

Soy-Ginger Glaze:

Prepare Glaze Mixture:

- In a small bowl, whisk together soy sauce, rice vinegar, maple syrup or agave nectar, sesame oil, grated ginger, and minced garlic.

Thicken with Cornstarch Slurry:
- In a separate bowl, mix 1 tablespoon of cornstarch with 2 tablespoons of water to create a cornstarch slurry. Stir the slurry into the soy-ginger mixture.

Simmer and Glaze:
- Pour the mixture into a saucepan and simmer over medium heat until it thickens to a glaze consistency. Remove from heat.

Coat Fried Tofu:
- Toss the crispy fried tofu in the soy-ginger glaze until evenly coated.

Garnish and Serve:
- Garnish with sesame seeds and chopped green onions. Serve the crispy fried tofu with the glaze on the side for dipping.

Tips:

- Adjust the sweetness and saltiness of the glaze to your taste by adding more maple syrup or soy sauce if needed.
- Serve over steamed rice or with stir-fried vegetables for a complete meal.

Enjoy this Crispy Fried Tofu with Soy-Ginger Glaze for a delicious and flavorful plant-based dish!

Spanish Churros with Chocolate Dipping Sauce

Ingredients:

For the Churros:

- 1 cup water
- 1/2 cup unsalted butter
- 1 tablespoon granulated sugar
- 1/4 teaspoon salt
- 1 cup all-purpose flour
- 3 large eggs
- Vegetable oil for frying

For the Cinnamon Sugar Coating:

- 1/2 cup granulated sugar
- 1 teaspoon ground cinnamon

For the Chocolate Dipping Sauce:

- 4 ounces dark chocolate, finely chopped
- 1/2 cup heavy cream
- 1 tablespoon unsalted butter
- 1/2 teaspoon vanilla extract

Instructions:

Churros:

    Prepare Dough:
- In a saucepan, combine water, butter, sugar, and salt. Bring to a boil over medium heat. Once boiling, remove from heat and stir in the flour until a smooth dough forms.

    Add Eggs:
- Add the eggs one at a time, mixing well after each addition, until the dough is smooth and sticky.

    Pipe Churros:

- Heat vegetable oil in a deep fryer or large pot to 375°F (190°C). Using a star tip, pipe the churro dough directly into the hot oil, cutting with scissors to your desired length.

Fry until Golden:
- Fry the churros until they are golden brown and crispy, turning them for even cooking. Remove with a slotted spoon and drain on paper towels.

Cinnamon Sugar Coating:

Coat in Cinnamon Sugar:
- In a bowl, mix granulated sugar and ground cinnamon. While the churros are still warm, roll them in the cinnamon sugar mixture until coated.

Chocolate Dipping Sauce:

Melt Chocolate:
- Place the finely chopped dark chocolate in a heatproof bowl. In a small saucepan, heat the heavy cream until it just begins to boil. Pour the hot cream over the chocolate and let it sit for a minute before stirring until smooth.

Add Butter and Vanilla:
- Stir in the butter and vanilla extract until well combined.

Serve:
- Serve the warm churros with the chocolate dipping sauce on the side.

Tips:

- The churro dough can also be piped into loops or spirals for variation.
- Adjust the thickness of the chocolate dipping sauce by adding more cream if desired.

Enjoy these Spanish Churros with Chocolate Dipping Sauce for a delightful treat!

Indian Pakoras with Mint Chutney

Ingredients:

For the Pakoras:

- 1 cup chickpea flour (besan)
- 1 medium-sized potato, peeled and thinly sliced
- 1 medium-sized onion, thinly sliced
- 1 cup spinach leaves, chopped
- 1/2 cup cilantro (coriander), chopped
- 1 teaspoon ginger, grated
- 1 teaspoon garlic, minced
- 1 teaspoon cumin seeds
- 1/2 teaspoon turmeric powder
- 1/2 teaspoon red chili powder
- Salt to taste
- Water, as needed
- Vegetable oil for frying

For the Mint Chutney:

- 1 cup fresh mint leaves
- 1/2 cup fresh cilantro (coriander) leaves
- 1 green chili, chopped
- 1 teaspoon ginger, grated
- 1 teaspoon garlic, minced
- 1 tablespoon lemon juice
- Salt to taste
- Water, as needed

Instructions:

Pakoras:

    Prepare Batter:
- In a bowl, mix chickpea flour, cumin seeds, turmeric powder, red chili powder, grated ginger, minced garlic, and salt. Gradually add water to make a thick batter.

    Add Vegetables:

- Add sliced potatoes, onions, chopped spinach, and cilantro to the batter. Mix until the vegetables are well coated.

Heat Oil:
- Heat vegetable oil in a deep fryer or large pot to 350°F (175°C).

Fry Pakoras:
- Drop spoonfuls of the batter into the hot oil and fry until the pakoras are golden brown and crispy. Remove with a slotted spoon and place on a plate lined with paper towels to drain excess oil.

Mint Chutney:

Blend Ingredients:
- In a blender, combine mint leaves, cilantro, chopped green chili, grated ginger, minced garlic, lemon juice, and salt. Blend until smooth, adding water as needed to reach the desired consistency.

Serve:
- Serve the pakoras hot with the mint chutney on the side for dipping.

Tips:

- You can customize the vegetables in the pakoras based on your preference.
- Adjust the spiciness of the mint chutney by adding more or fewer green chilies.

Enjoy these delicious Indian Pakoras with Mint Chutney as a flavorful snack or appetizer!

Potato Latkes with Applesauce

Ingredients:

For the Potato Latkes:

- 4 large potatoes, peeled
- 1 onion
- 2 eggs, beaten
- 3 tablespoons all-purpose flour
- 1 teaspoon salt
- 1/2 teaspoon black pepper
- Vegetable oil, for frying

For the Applesauce:

- 4 apples, peeled, cored, and chopped
- 1/4 cup water
- 2 tablespoons sugar (adjust to taste)
- 1/2 teaspoon cinnamon

Instructions:

Potato Latkes:

- Grate Potatoes and Onion:
    - Use a box grater to grate the potatoes and onion. Place them in a clean kitchen towel and squeeze out excess moisture.
- Mix Batter:
    - In a large bowl, combine the grated potatoes and onion with beaten eggs, flour, salt, and black pepper. Mix well to form a batter.
- Heat Oil:
    - Heat vegetable oil in a large skillet over medium-high heat.
- Fry Latkes:

- Drop spoonfuls of the batter into the hot oil, pressing them down with a spatula to form flat pancakes. Fry until the edges are golden brown, then flip and cook the other side.

Drain Excess Oil:
- Place the cooked latkes on a plate lined with paper towels to drain excess oil.

Applesauce:

Cook Apples:
- In a saucepan, combine chopped apples, water, sugar, and cinnamon. Cook over medium heat until the apples are soft and can be easily mashed with a fork.

Mash Apples:
- Mash the cooked apples with a fork or potato masher to achieve the desired applesauce consistency.

Adjust Sweetness:
- Taste the applesauce and adjust the sweetness by adding more sugar if needed.

Serve:

- Serve the potato latkes hot, topped with a dollop of applesauce on the side.

Tips:

- Keep the latkes warm in the oven while frying batches.
- Experiment with different types of apples for varied flavors in the applesauce.

Enjoy these crispy Potato Latkes with a side of homemade Applesauce for a delightful and classic combination!

Szechuan Orange Chicken

Ingredients:

For the Orange Sauce:

- 1/2 cup orange juice
- 1/4 cup soy sauce
- 2 tablespoons rice vinegar
- 2 tablespoons honey
- 1 tablespoon cornstarch
- 1 teaspoon sesame oil
- 1 teaspoon grated orange zest
- 1/2 teaspoon crushed red pepper flakes (adjust to taste)

For the Chicken:

- 1.5 lbs boneless, skinless chicken breasts, cut into bite-sized pieces
- Salt and black pepper to taste
- 1 cup cornstarch for coating
- Vegetable oil for frying
- 3 cloves garlic, minced
- 1 tablespoon fresh ginger, grated
- 1 bell pepper, sliced
- 2 green onions, sliced (for garnish)
- Sesame seeds (optional, for garnish)

Instructions:

Orange Sauce:

> Mix Ingredients:
> - In a bowl, whisk together orange juice, soy sauce, rice vinegar, honey, cornstarch, sesame oil, orange zest, and crushed red pepper flakes. Set aside.

Chicken:

Season Chicken:
- Season the chicken pieces with salt and black pepper. Coat them evenly with cornstarch.

Fry Chicken:
- Heat vegetable oil in a large skillet or wok over medium-high heat. Fry the coated chicken until golden brown and crispy. Remove and place on a plate lined with paper towels.

Sauté Vegetables:
- In the same skillet, sauté minced garlic, grated ginger, and sliced bell pepper until they are slightly tender.

Add Sauce:
- Pour the prepared orange sauce into the skillet. Stir well and let it simmer until the sauce thickens.

Combine Chicken:
- Add the fried chicken back into the skillet, tossing to coat each piece evenly with the sauce.

Garnish and Serve:
- Garnish with sliced green onions and sesame seeds if desired. Serve the Szechuan Orange Chicken over rice or noodles.

Tips:

- Adjust the level of spiciness by varying the amount of crushed red pepper flakes.
- For an extra kick, you can add a splash of hot chili oil to the sauce.

Enjoy this flavorful and zesty Szechuan Orange Chicken as a delicious main dish!

Fried Ravioli with Marinara

Ingredients:

For the Fried Ravioli:

- 1 package of fresh or frozen cheese ravioli
- 2 cups Italian-style breadcrumbs
- 1 cup grated Parmesan cheese
- 3 large eggs, beaten
- Vegetable oil for frying

For the Marinara Sauce:

- 2 cups crushed tomatoes
- 1/4 cup olive oil
- 3 cloves garlic, minced
- 1 teaspoon dried oregano
- 1 teaspoon dried basil
- Salt and black pepper to taste
- Fresh basil leaves for garnish (optional)

Instructions:

Fried Ravioli:

Prepare Breading Station:
- Set up a breading station with one bowl containing the beaten eggs, another bowl with a mixture of breadcrumbs and Parmesan cheese.

Bread Ravioli:
- Dip each ravioli into the beaten eggs, ensuring it's fully coated. Then, dredge it in the breadcrumb and Parmesan mixture, pressing gently to adhere the coating.

Heat Oil:
- In a large skillet, heat vegetable oil over medium-high heat.

Fry Ravioli:

- Fry the breaded ravioli in batches until golden brown and crispy, approximately 2-3 minutes per side. Place the fried ravioli on a plate lined with paper towels to absorb excess oil.

Marinara Sauce:

Sauté Garlic:
- In a saucepan, heat olive oil over medium heat. Add minced garlic and sauté until fragrant.

Add Crushed Tomatoes:
- Pour in the crushed tomatoes, dried oregano, dried basil, salt, and black pepper. Stir to combine.

Simmer:
- Let the sauce simmer for 15-20 minutes, allowing the flavors to meld and the sauce to thicken.

Serve:
- Serve the fried ravioli with marinara sauce for dipping. Garnish with fresh basil leaves if desired.

Tips:

- Experiment with different types of ravioli, such as spinach and ricotta or meat-filled, for variety.
- Make sure the oil is hot enough to achieve a crispy texture on the ravioli.

Enjoy this Fried Ravioli with Marinara as a delightful appetizer or snack!

Homemade Corn Dogs with Mustard

Ingredients:

For the Corn Dogs:

- 1 cup yellow cornmeal
- 1 cup all-purpose flour
- 1/4 cup granulated sugar
- 1 tablespoon baking powder
- 1/4 teaspoon salt
- 1 cup buttermilk
- 1/4 cup unsalted butter, melted
- 1 large egg
- 8-10 hot dogs
- Wooden skewers or popsicle sticks
- Vegetable oil, for frying

For the Mustard Sauce:

- 1/2 cup yellow mustard
- 2 tablespoons mayonnaise
- 1 tablespoon honey
- Pinch of salt

Instructions:

Corn Dogs:

> Prepare Batter:
> - In a bowl, whisk together cornmeal, flour, sugar, baking powder, and salt. Add buttermilk, melted butter, and the egg. Mix until smooth.
>
> Skewer Hot Dogs:
> - Insert wooden skewers or popsicle sticks into each hot dog, leaving enough space to hold onto.
>
> Coat Hot Dogs:
> - Dip each hot dog into the batter, ensuring an even coating.

Fry Corn Dogs:
- Heat vegetable oil in a deep pan or fryer to 350°F (175°C). Carefully place the coated hot dogs into the hot oil and fry until golden brown, turning to cook all sides. This should take about 3-5 minutes.

Drain Excess Oil:
- Remove the corn dogs from the oil and place them on a plate lined with paper towels to drain any excess oil.

Mustard Sauce:

Mix Ingredients:
- In a small bowl, whisk together yellow mustard, mayonnaise, honey, and a pinch of salt until well combined.

Serve:
- Serve the homemade corn dogs with the mustard sauce for dipping.

Tips:

- Make sure the oil is at the right temperature to achieve a crispy and golden exterior on the corn dogs.
- Customize the mustard sauce by adjusting the honey or adding a dash of hot sauce for extra flavor.

Enjoy these Homemade Corn Dogs with Mustard as a nostalgic and tasty treat!

Buttermilk Fried Oysters with Lemon Aioli

Ingredients:

For the Fried Oysters:

- 1 dozen fresh oysters, shucked
- 1 cup buttermilk
- 1 cup all-purpose flour
- 1 teaspoon Old Bay seasoning
- 1/2 teaspoon garlic powder
- Salt and black pepper to taste
- Vegetable oil, for frying

For the Lemon Aioli:

- 1/2 cup mayonnaise
- 1 tablespoon fresh lemon juice
- 1 teaspoon lemon zest
- 1 clove garlic, minced
- Salt and black pepper to taste
- Chopped fresh parsley for garnish (optional)

Instructions:

Fried Oysters:

    Marinate Oysters:
- Place the shucked oysters in a bowl and pour buttermilk over them. Let them marinate for at least 30 minutes, allowing the buttermilk to impart flavor and tenderize the oysters.

    Prepare Coating:
- In a separate bowl, combine flour, Old Bay seasoning, garlic powder, salt, and black pepper.

    Coat Oysters:
- Remove the oysters from the buttermilk, letting excess liquid drain off. Dredge each oyster in the seasoned flour mixture, ensuring an even coating.

    Fry Oysters:

- Heat vegetable oil in a deep fryer or large skillet to 350°F (175°C). Carefully fry the oysters in batches until they are golden brown and crispy, approximately 2-3 minutes per batch. Place them on a plate lined with paper towels to absorb any excess oil.

Lemon Aioli:

Mix Ingredients:
- In a small bowl, whisk together mayonnaise, fresh lemon juice, lemon zest, minced garlic, salt, and black pepper.

Serve:
- Serve the buttermilk fried oysters hot, with the lemon aioli on the side for dipping. Garnish with chopped fresh parsley if desired.

Tips:

- Adjust the seasoning in the flour mixture according to your preference.
- For an extra kick, you can add a pinch of cayenne pepper to the flour mixture.

Enjoy these Buttermilk Fried Oysters with Lemon Aioli as a delicious appetizer or seafood treat!

Coconut-Crusted Banana Fritters

Ingredients:

For the Banana Fritters:

- 3 ripe bananas
- 1 cup all-purpose flour
- 2 tablespoons sugar
- 1 teaspoon baking powder
- 1/2 teaspoon cinnamon
- 1/4 teaspoon salt
- 1/2 cup coconut milk
- 1 teaspoon vanilla extract
- Vegetable oil, for frying

For the Coconut Coating:

- 1 cup shredded coconut (sweetened or unsweetened)

For the Maple Drizzle (Optional):

- Maple syrup
- Chopped nuts for garnish (optional)

Instructions:

Banana Fritters:

Prepare Bananas:
- Peel and mash the ripe bananas in a bowl.

Prepare Batter:
- In a separate bowl, whisk together flour, sugar, baking powder, cinnamon, and salt.

Combine Ingredients:
- Add the mashed bananas, coconut milk, and vanilla extract to the dry ingredients. Stir until well combined, creating a thick batter.

Heat Oil:
- Heat vegetable oil in a deep pan or fryer to 350°F (175°C).

Form Fritters:

- Drop spoonfuls of the batter into the shredded coconut, coating the fritters on all sides.

Fry Fritters:
- Fry the coconut-coated banana fritters in batches until they are golden brown and crispy, about 2-3 minutes per side. Place them on a plate lined with paper towels to absorb excess oil.

Maple Drizzle (Optional):

Drizzle with Maple Syrup:
- If desired, drizzle the coconut-crusted banana fritters with maple syrup just before serving.

Garnish (Optional):
- Optionally, garnish with chopped nuts for added texture and flavor.

Tips:

- Experiment with the level of sweetness by adjusting the amount of sugar in the batter.
- Serve the fritters warm for the best flavor and texture.

Enjoy these Coconut-Crusted Banana Fritters as a delightful dessert or snack!

General Tso's Cauliflower

Ingredients:

For the Cauliflower:

- 1 large cauliflower, cut into bite-sized florets
- 1 cup all-purpose flour
- 1 cup cornstarch
- 1 teaspoon baking powder
- 1 teaspoon salt
- 1 cup water
- Vegetable oil, for frying

For the General Tso's Sauce:

- 1/4 cup soy sauce
- 3 tablespoons hoisin sauce
- 2 tablespoons rice vinegar
- 2 tablespoons brown sugar
- 1 tablespoon cornstarch
- 1 teaspoon sesame oil
- 1 teaspoon ginger, minced
- 2 cloves garlic, minced
- 1/2 teaspoon red pepper flakes (adjust to taste)
- 1 cup water
- Green onions and sesame seeds for garnish (optional)

Instructions:

Cauliflower:

> Prepare Batter:
> - In a bowl, whisk together flour, cornstarch, baking powder, salt, and water to create a thick batter.
>
> Coat Cauliflower:
> - Dip each cauliflower floret into the batter, ensuring an even coating.
>
> Fry Cauliflower:
> - Heat vegetable oil in a deep pan or fryer to 375°F (190°C). Fry the battered cauliflower in batches until they are golden brown and crispy, about 3-4

minutes per batch. Place them on a plate lined with paper towels to absorb excess oil.

General Tso's Sauce:

Mix Ingredients:
- In a small bowl, whisk together soy sauce, hoisin sauce, rice vinegar, brown sugar, cornstarch, sesame oil, ginger, garlic, red pepper flakes, and water.

Cook Sauce:
- Pour the sauce into a saucepan and bring it to a simmer over medium heat. Stir continuously until the sauce thickens.

Coat Cauliflower:
- Toss the fried cauliflower in the General Tso's sauce until evenly coated.

Garnish (Optional):
- Garnish with chopped green onions and sesame seeds if desired.

Serve General Tso's Cauliflower over rice or as a delicious appetizer!

Tips:

- Adjust the level of spiciness by varying the amount of red pepper flakes in the sauce.
- Make sure the cauliflower is well-drained after frying to prevent sogginess.

Crab Rangoon with Sweet and Sour Sauce

Ingredients:

For the Crab Rangoon:

- 8 oz (about 1 cup) canned crab meat, drained
- 8 oz cream cheese, softened
- 2 green onions, finely chopped
- 1 clove garlic, minced
- 1/2 teaspoon Worcestershire sauce
- 1/4 teaspoon soy sauce
- 1/4 teaspoon salt
- 1/8 teaspoon black pepper
- 1 package wonton wrappers
- Vegetable oil, for frying

For the Sweet and Sour Sauce:

- 1/2 cup pineapple juice
- 1/4 cup rice vinegar
- 3 tablespoons ketchup
- 2 tablespoons brown sugar
- 1 tablespoon soy sauce
- 1 tablespoon cornstarch
- 1/4 cup water

Instructions:

Crab Rangoon:

    Prepare Filling:
- In a bowl, combine drained crab meat, cream cheese, green onions, garlic, Worcestershire sauce, soy sauce, salt, and black pepper. Mix until well combined.

    Assemble Crab Rangoon:

- Place a small spoonful of the crab mixture in the center of each wonton wrapper. Moisten the edges with water and fold the wrapper in half to form a triangle. Press the edges to seal, ensuring no air is trapped inside.

Heat Oil:
- Heat vegetable oil in a deep pan or fryer to 350°F (175°C).

Fry Crab Rangoon:
- Fry the crab rangoon in batches until they are golden brown and crispy, about 2-3 minutes per batch. Place them on a plate lined with paper towels to absorb excess oil.

Sweet and Sour Sauce:

Mix Ingredients:
- In a saucepan, combine pineapple juice, rice vinegar, ketchup, brown sugar, and soy sauce.

Create Cornstarch Slurry:
- In a small bowl, mix cornstarch and water to create a slurry. Add the slurry to the saucepan.

Cook Sauce:
- Bring the sauce to a simmer over medium heat, stirring continuously until it thickens.

Serve:
- Serve the crab rangoon with the sweet and sour sauce on the side for dipping.

Tips:

- Ensure the oil is at the right temperature before frying to achieve a crispy texture.
- You can customize the filling by adding a touch of hot sauce or ginger for extra flavor.

Enjoy your homemade Crab Rangoon with Sweet and Sour Sauce!

Fried Avocado Tacos with Lime Crema

Ingredients:

For the Fried Avocado:

- 2 avocados, sliced
- 1 cup all-purpose flour
- 2 large eggs, beaten
- 1 cup breadcrumbs
- 1 teaspoon chili powder
- 1/2 teaspoon garlic powder
- 1/2 teaspoon cumin
- Salt and pepper to taste
- Vegetable oil for frying

For the Lime Crema:

- 1/2 cup sour cream
- Juice of 1 lime
- 1 teaspoon lime zest
- Salt and pepper to taste

For the Tacos:

- Corn or flour tortillas
- Shredded lettuce
- Diced tomatoes
- Sliced red onions
- Fresh cilantro, chopped
- Lime wedges for serving

Instructions:

Fried Avocado:

    Prepare Avocado Slices:

- Peel and slice the avocados.

Set up Breading Station:
- In three separate bowls, place flour in one, beaten eggs in another, and a mixture of breadcrumbs, chili powder, garlic powder, cumin, salt, and pepper in the third.

Bread Avocado Slices:
- Dip each avocado slice in the flour, then the beaten eggs, and finally the breadcrumb mixture, ensuring each slice is coated evenly.

Fry Avocado:
- Heat vegetable oil in a pan over medium-high heat. Fry the breaded avocado slices until golden brown on each side. Place them on a paper towel-lined plate to absorb excess oil.

Lime Crema:

Prepare Crema:
- In a bowl, whisk together sour cream, lime juice, lime zest, salt, and pepper.

Assemble Tacos:

Warm Tortillas:
- Heat the tortillas in a dry skillet or microwave until warm.

Assemble Tacos:
- Spread a spoonful of lime crema on each tortilla. Add fried avocado slices and top with shredded lettuce, diced tomatoes, sliced red onions, and chopped cilantro.

Serve:
- Serve the tacos with lime wedges on the side.

Tips:

- Customize the toppings based on your preferences, adding salsa, cheese, or hot sauce.
- If you prefer a spicier crema, add a pinch of cayenne pepper or hot sauce.

Enjoy these delicious Fried Avocado Tacos with Lime Crema!

Jamaican Festival Dumplings

Ingredients:

- 2 cups all-purpose flour
- 1/4 cup cornmeal
- 1/4 cup sugar
- 1 teaspoon baking powder
- 1/4 teaspoon salt
- 1/2 cup cold water (or more as needed)
- Vegetable oil for frying

Instructions:

Mix Dry Ingredients:
- In a large bowl, combine the all-purpose flour, cornmeal, sugar, baking powder, and salt. Mix well to ensure even distribution of dry ingredients.

Form Dough:
- Gradually add cold water to the dry ingredients, stirring continuously, until a soft and slightly sticky dough forms. You may need to adjust the amount of water based on the consistency of the dough.

Knead Dough:
- Turn the dough out onto a floured surface and knead it for a few minutes until it becomes smooth and elastic.

Shape Dumplings:
- Pinch off small portions of the dough and roll them into oval-shaped dumplings, about 3-4 inches long. You can shape them into rounds or cylinders as well.

Heat Oil:
- In a deep pan or fryer, heat vegetable oil to 350°F (175°C).

Fry Dumplings:
- Carefully add the shaped dumplings to the hot oil, frying in batches. Ensure they are fully submerged in the oil. Fry until they are golden brown and crispy on the outside, turning occasionally for even cooking.

Drain Excess Oil:
- Once fried, use a slotted spoon to remove the festival dumplings from the oil and place them on a plate lined with paper towels to drain any excess oil.

Serve:
- Serve the Jamaican Festival Dumplings warm. They are often enjoyed on their own or served alongside jerk chicken, fish, or other Jamaican dishes.

Tips:

- Adjust the sugar quantity according to your preference for sweetness.
- The dough should be soft but not too sticky; add more flour if needed during kneading.

Enjoy your homemade Jamaican Festival Dumplings!

Crispy Fried Egg Rolls with Sweet Chili Sauce

Ingredients:

For the Egg Rolls:

- 1 cup finely shredded cabbage
- 1 cup julienned carrots
- 1 cup bean sprouts
- 1 cup finely chopped cooked chicken or shrimp (optional)
- 2 green onions, finely chopped
- 2 cloves garlic, minced
- 1 teaspoon ginger, grated
- 2 tablespoons soy sauce
- 1 tablespoon oyster sauce
- 1 teaspoon sesame oil
- 1 package egg roll wrappers (about 12-16 wrappers)
- Vegetable oil for frying

For the Sweet Chili Sauce:

- 1/2 cup sweet chili sauce
- 1 tablespoon soy sauce
- 1 teaspoon rice vinegar
- 1 teaspoon sesame oil (optional)

Instructions:

Prepare the Filling:

    Mix Vegetables:
- In a large bowl, combine shredded cabbage, julienned carrots, bean sprouts, chopped chicken or shrimp (if using), green onions, garlic, and ginger.

    Season Filling:
- Add soy sauce, oyster sauce, and sesame oil to the vegetable mixture. Toss well to combine and coat the ingredients with the seasonings.

Assemble and Roll:

Wrap Egg Rolls:
- Place an egg roll wrapper on a clean surface with one corner pointing towards you. Spoon a portion of the filling onto the center of the wrapper.

Roll and Seal:
- Fold the bottom corner over the filling, then fold in the sides, and roll it up tightly. Use a bit of water on the edges to seal the wrapper.

Repeat:
- Repeat the process with the remaining wrappers and filling.

Fry the Egg Rolls:

Heat Oil:
- In a deep pan or fryer, heat vegetable oil to 350°F (175°C).

Fry Egg Rolls:
- Carefully place the rolled egg rolls into the hot oil, a few at a time. Fry until they are golden brown and crispy, turning occasionally for even cooking.

Drain Excess Oil:
- Once fried, use a slotted spoon to remove the egg rolls from the oil and place them on a plate lined with paper towels to drain any excess oil.

Prepare Sweet Chili Sauce:

Mix Sauce:
- In a small bowl, mix together sweet chili sauce, soy sauce, rice vinegar, and sesame oil (if using).

Serve:

Serve Warm:
- Serve the crispy fried egg rolls warm with the prepared sweet chili sauce for dipping.

Tips:

- Customize the filling with your favorite vegetables and protein.
- Ensure the oil is hot enough for a crispy texture, but be cautious not to overheat.

Enjoy your delicious Crispy Fried Egg Rolls with Sweet Chili Sauce!

Cajun Fried Turkey for a Festive Twist

Ingredients:

For the Cajun Rub:

- 2 tablespoons paprika
- 1 tablespoon onion powder
- 1 tablespoon garlic powder
- 1 tablespoon dried thyme
- 1 tablespoon dried oregano
- 1 tablespoon cayenne pepper (adjust to taste for spice level)
- 1 tablespoon black pepper
- 1 tablespoon white pepper
- 1 tablespoon salt

For the Turkey:

- 1 whole turkey (12-14 pounds), thawed
- 3 gallons peanut oil (or other high smoke point oil)

Instructions:

Prepare the Cajun Rub:

Mix Spices:
- In a bowl, thoroughly mix together paprika, onion powder, garlic powder, dried thyme, dried oregano, cayenne pepper, black pepper, white pepper, and salt to create the Cajun rub.

Prepare the Turkey:

Dry the Turkey:
- Pat the turkey dry with paper towels inside and out.

Apply Cajun Rub:
- Rub the Cajun seasoning mixture all over the turkey, making sure to get it under the skin and inside the cavity. Allow the seasoned turkey to sit at room temperature for about 30 minutes to let the flavors infuse.

Heat Oil:

- In a large turkey fryer, heat the peanut oil to 350°F (175°C). Ensure that the oil level is below the maximum fill line.

Fry the Turkey:

- Carefully lower the turkey into the hot oil using the fryer basket or turkey hook. Fry the turkey for about 3 to 4 minutes per pound or until the internal temperature reaches 165°F (74°C).

Monitor Temperature:

- Use a meat thermometer to check the internal temperature at the thickest part of the thigh and the breast. Avoid letting the thermometer touch the bone.

Remove and Drain:

- Once the turkey reaches the desired temperature, carefully remove it from the oil and let it drain on a rack or paper towels.

Rest and Carve:

- Allow the turkey to rest for about 20 minutes before carving. This helps the juices redistribute for a moist and flavorful result.

Serve:

- Carve and serve the Cajun Fried Turkey as the centerpiece for your festive celebration.

Tips:

- Ensure the turkey is completely thawed and dry before frying to avoid splattering.
- Use caution when lowering and lifting the turkey into and out of the hot oil.

Enjoy your Cajun Fried Turkey with a festive Cajun twist!

Cheddar Jalapeño Hush Puppies

Ingredients:

- 1 cup yellow cornmeal
- 1/2 cup all-purpose flour
- 1 teaspoon baking powder
- 1/2 teaspoon baking soda
- 1/2 teaspoon salt
- 1/2 cup buttermilk
- 1 large egg, beaten
- 1 cup sharp cheddar cheese, shredded
- 1/4 cup green onions, finely chopped
- 1-2 jalapeños, finely chopped (adjust to taste, and remove seeds for less heat)
- Vegetable oil for frying

Instructions:

Prepare Batter:
- In a mixing bowl, whisk together cornmeal, flour, baking powder, baking soda, and salt.

Add Wet Ingredients:
- Pour in buttermilk and beaten egg. Stir until just combined. The batter should be thick but moist.

Add Cheese and Flavorings:
- Fold in shredded cheddar cheese, chopped green onions, and chopped jalapeños into the batter.

Heat Oil:
- In a deep pot or fryer, heat enough vegetable oil to 350°F (175°C).

Drop into Hot Oil:
- Using a spoon or a small ice cream scoop, drop portions of the batter into the hot oil. Fry in batches to avoid overcrowding.

Fry Until Golden:
- Fry the hush puppies for about 2-3 minutes or until they are golden brown and cooked through. Use a slotted spoon to turn them for even cooking.

Drain and Serve:
- Remove the hush puppies from the oil and place them on a plate lined with paper towels to drain any excess oil.

Repeat:

- Continue frying the remaining batches until all the batter is used.

Serve:

- Serve the Cheddar Jalapeño Hush Puppies warm as a delightful side dish or snack.

Tips:

- Adjust the amount of jalapeños to suit your spice preference.
- Serve with a dipping sauce like ranch dressing or a spicy mayo for extra flavor.

Enjoy your flavorful Cheddar Jalapeño Hush Puppies!

Italian Arancini Stuffed with Mozzarella

Ingredients:

For the Risotto:

- 1 cup Arborio rice
- 1/2 cup dry white wine
- 4 cups chicken or vegetable broth, kept warm
- 1 small onion, finely chopped
- 2 cloves garlic, minced
- 1/2 cup grated Parmesan cheese
- Salt and pepper to taste
- Olive oil for sautéing

For the Arancini:

- Fresh mozzarella cheese, cut into small cubes
- 2 cups breadcrumbs
- 3 large eggs, beaten
- Vegetable oil for frying

Instructions:

Prepare Risotto:

    Sauté Onions and Garlic:
- In a large pan, sauté chopped onions in olive oil until translucent. Add minced garlic and cook for an additional minute.

    Cook Rice:
- Add Arborio rice to the pan and cook for 1-2 minutes, allowing the rice to toast slightly.

    Deglaze with Wine:
- Pour in the white wine and stir until it's mostly absorbed by the rice.

    Add Broth:
- Begin adding the warm broth one ladle at a time. Allow each ladle to be absorbed before adding the next. Continue until the rice is creamy and cooked al dente.

    Season and Add Cheese:

- Stir in the grated Parmesan cheese, and season with salt and pepper. Let the risotto cool.

Assemble Arancini:

Shape Risotto Balls:
- Take a small portion of the cooled risotto in your hand, flatten it, place a cube of mozzarella in the center, and encase the cheese with the rice, forming a ball.

Coat in Breadcrumbs:
- Dip each rice ball into the beaten eggs and then roll in breadcrumbs until well coated. Repeat for all the arancini.

Fry Arancini:

Heat Oil:
- In a deep fryer or heavy pot, heat vegetable oil to 350°F (175°C).

Fry Until Golden:
- Carefully lower the arancini into the hot oil and fry until they are golden brown and crispy on the outside.

Drain and Serve:
- Use a slotted spoon to remove the arancini from the oil and place them on a plate lined with paper towels to drain any excess oil.

Serve:

- Serve the Italian Arancini warm, and optionally with marinara sauce for dipping.

Tips:

- Make sure the risotto is well-cooled before shaping the arancini to make it easier to handle.
- Experiment with different cheese fillings or add herbs to the risotto for additional flavor.

Enjoy your delicious Italian Arancini Stuffed with Mozzarella!

Tempura Vegetables with Ponzu Sauce

Ingredients:

For Tempura Batter:

- 1 cup all-purpose flour
- 1 cup ice-cold water
- 1 egg, beaten
- Ice cubes

For Tempura Vegetables:

- Assorted vegetables (e.g., zucchini, sweet potatoes, bell peppers, broccoli florets)
- Vegetable oil for frying
- Salt for seasoning

For Ponzu Sauce:

- 1/4 cup soy sauce
- 2 tablespoons freshly squeezed lemon juice
- 1 tablespoon rice vinegar
- 1 tablespoon mirin (optional)
- 1 teaspoon grated daikon radish (optional)
- 1 teaspoon finely chopped green onions (optional)

Instructions:

Prepare Ponzu Sauce:

  Mix Ingredients:
  - In a small bowl, whisk together soy sauce, lemon juice, rice vinegar, mirin (if using), grated daikon radish, and chopped green onions. Set aside.

Prepare Tempura Batter:

  Keep Ingredients Cold:
  - Place a large bowl over another bowl filled with ice cubes. Ensure the water is cold.

Make Batter:
- In the large bowl, combine flour, ice-cold water, and beaten egg. Mix gently until just combined. It's okay if there are lumps; do not overmix.

Cook Tempura Vegetables:

Prepare Vegetables:
- Cut the vegetables into bite-sized pieces.

Heat Oil:
- In a deep fryer or a large, deep pot, heat vegetable oil to 350°F (175°C).

Coat Vegetables:
- Dip the vegetables into the tempura batter, ensuring they are well coated.

Fry Until Golden:
- Carefully place the coated vegetables into the hot oil. Fry until they turn golden brown and crispy. Fry in batches to avoid overcrowding.

Drain and Season:
- Use a slotted spoon to remove the tempura vegetables and place them on a plate lined with paper towels. Immediately sprinkle with a pinch of salt.

Serve:

- Serve the Tempura Vegetables hot with the Ponzu Sauce for dipping.

Tips:

- Use a variety of colorful vegetables for a visually appealing dish.
- Adjust the Ponzu Sauce ingredients to your taste preference, adding more lemon juice or soy sauce if needed.

Enjoy your delightful Tempura Vegetables with Ponzu Sauce!

Beer-Battered Onion Petals

Ingredients:

For Beer Batter:

- 1 cup all-purpose flour
- 1 cup cold beer (light beer works well)
- 1 teaspoon baking powder
- 1/2 teaspoon salt
- 1/2 teaspoon paprika
- 1/4 teaspoon black pepper
- Vegetable oil for frying

For Onion Petals:

- 1 large onion, peeled and cut into petals
- Additional flour for coating the onion petals
- Salt and pepper for seasoning

Instructions:

Prepare Beer Batter:

 Mix Ingredients:
- In a bowl, whisk together the flour, cold beer, baking powder, salt, paprika, and black pepper. The batter should be smooth but not overmixed.

 Chill Batter:
- Allow the batter to rest in the refrigerator for about 15-30 minutes. This helps create a crispier coating.

Prepare Onion Petals:

 Separate Onion Petals:
- Carefully peel the onion and separate it into individual petals.

 Coat in Flour:

- Lightly coat the onion petals in additional flour. This helps the batter adhere to the onions.

Fry Onion Petals:

Heat Oil:
- In a deep fryer or a large, deep pot, heat vegetable oil to 350°F (175°C).

Dip in Batter:
- Dip each flour-coated onion petal into the chilled beer batter, ensuring it is well-coated.

Fry Until Golden:
- Carefully place the battered onion petals into the hot oil. Fry until they turn golden brown and crispy. Fry in batches to avoid overcrowding.

Drain and Season:
- Use a slotted spoon to remove the beer-battered onion petals and place them on a plate lined with paper towels. Immediately sprinkle with salt and pepper.

Serve:

- Serve the Beer-Battered Onion Petals hot with your favorite dipping sauce, such as spicy mayo or ranch.

Tips:

- Adjust the seasoning in the beer batter according to your taste preference.
- Experiment with different dipping sauces for added flavor variety.

Enjoy your delicious Beer-Battered Onion Petals!

Shrimp Po' Boy Sandwiches with Remoulade

Ingredients:

For Shrimp:

- 1 pound large shrimp, peeled and deveined
- 1 cup buttermilk
- 1 cup cornmeal
- 1 cup all-purpose flour
- 1 teaspoon salt
- 1/2 teaspoon black pepper
- Vegetable oil for frying

For Remoulade Sauce:

- 1 cup mayonnaise
- 2 tablespoons Dijon mustard
- 1 tablespoon hot sauce
- 1 tablespoon capers, chopped
- 2 green onions, finely chopped
- 1 clove garlic, minced
- 1 tablespoon fresh parsley, chopped
- Salt and pepper to taste

For Sandwiches:

- French bread or baguette, cut into sandwich-sized pieces
- Shredded lettuce
- Sliced tomatoes
- Sliced pickles

Instructions:

Prepare Remoulade Sauce:

Mix Ingredients:
- In a bowl, whisk together mayonnaise, Dijon mustard, hot sauce, chopped capers, green onions, minced garlic, chopped parsley, salt, and pepper. Refrigerate until ready to use.

Prepare Shrimp:

- Marinate Shrimp:
  - Place shrimp in a bowl and pour buttermilk over them. Let them marinate for at least 30 minutes.
- Prepare Coating:
  - In a shallow dish, combine cornmeal, flour, salt, and black pepper.
- Coat Shrimp:
  - Heat vegetable oil in a deep fryer or large pot to 350°F (175°C). Dredge each shrimp in the cornmeal mixture, ensuring they are well-coated.
- Fry Shrimp:
  - Fry the shrimp in batches until golden brown and cooked through, about 2-3 minutes per batch. Remove with a slotted spoon and drain on paper towels.

Assemble Po' Boy Sandwiches:

- Prepare Bread:
  - Cut the French bread or baguette into sandwich-sized pieces.
- Spread Remoulade:
  - Spread a generous amount of the prepared remoulade sauce on each side of the bread.
- Layer Ingredients:
  - On the bottom half of the bread, layer shredded lettuce, sliced tomatoes, pickles, and the fried shrimp.
- Close and Serve:
  - Place the other half of the bread on top to close the sandwich. Serve immediately.

Tips:

- Customize your Po' Boy with additional toppings like sliced onions, hot sauce, or coleslaw.
- Adjust the spiciness of the remoulade sauce by modifying the amount of hot sauce used.

Enjoy your flavorful Shrimp Po' Boy Sandwiches with Remoulade!

Fried Banana Spring Rolls with Caramel Sauce

Ingredients:

For Banana Filling:

- 4 ripe bananas, peeled and sliced
- 1/4 cup brown sugar
- 1 teaspoon ground cinnamon
- 1/4 teaspoon nutmeg (optional)
- Spring roll wrappers (rice paper or egg roll wrappers)

For Caramel Sauce:

- 1/2 cup granulated sugar
- 1/4 cup water
- 1/4 cup unsalted butter
- 1/4 cup heavy cream
- 1 teaspoon vanilla extract

For Frying:

- Vegetable oil for frying

Instructions:

Prepare Banana Filling:

   Mix Ingredients:
   - In a bowl, combine sliced bananas, brown sugar, ground cinnamon, and nutmeg. Toss until bananas are well coated.

   Assemble Spring Rolls:
   - Place a spring roll wrapper on a clean surface. Add a portion of the banana filling near one edge of the wrapper. Roll the wrapper tightly over the filling, folding in the sides as you roll. Seal the edge with a bit of water. Repeat for all spring rolls.

Prepare Caramel Sauce:

   Cook Sugar and Water:

- In a saucepan, combine granulated sugar and water over medium heat. Stir until the sugar dissolves. Allow the mixture to come to a boil without stirring.

Caramelize Sugar:
- Continue boiling until the mixture turns a deep amber color. Swirl the pan occasionally to ensure even caramelization.

Add Butter and Cream:
- Carefully add butter to the caramel, stirring until melted. Remove the pan from heat and slowly pour in the heavy cream while stirring. Be cautious as the mixture will bubble.

Finish with Vanilla:
- Stir in vanilla extract. Allow the caramel sauce to cool slightly.

Fry Banana Spring Rolls:

Heat Oil:
- Heat vegetable oil in a deep fryer or a large, deep pan to 350°F (175°C).

Fry Spring Rolls:
- Carefully place the banana spring rolls in the hot oil and fry until golden brown, about 3-4 minutes. Fry in batches, if necessary.

Drain and Cool:
- Remove the spring rolls with a slotted spoon and place them on a paper towel-lined plate to drain excess oil.

Serve with Caramel Sauce:
- Serve the fried banana spring rolls warm, drizzled with the prepared caramel sauce.

Tips:

- Dust the spring rolls with powdered sugar or cinnamon for an extra touch.
- Serve with a scoop of vanilla ice cream for a delightful dessert.

Enjoy your Fried Banana Spring Rolls with Caramel Sauce!

Greek Spanakopita Triangles

Ingredients:

For Filling:

- 1 pound fresh spinach, washed and chopped
- 1 cup feta cheese, crumbled
- 1 cup ricotta cheese
- 1/2 cup Parmesan cheese, grated
- 1 small onion, finely chopped
- 2 cloves garlic, minced
- 1 tablespoon olive oil
- 1 teaspoon dried oregano
- Salt and pepper to taste

For Assembly:

- 1 package phyllo dough, thawed
- 1/2 cup unsalted butter, melted
- Olive oil for brushing

Instructions:

Prepare Filling:

 Saute Spinach:
- In a large skillet, heat olive oil over medium heat. Add chopped onions and garlic, sauté until softened. Add chopped spinach and cook until wilted. Allow the mixture to cool.

 Mix Ingredients:
- In a bowl, combine the cooled spinach mixture with feta cheese, ricotta cheese, Parmesan cheese, dried oregano, salt, and pepper. Mix well.

Assemble Spanakopita Triangles:

 Preheat Oven:
- Preheat the oven to 375°F (190°C).

 Prepare Phyllo Dough:

- Lay out one sheet of phyllo dough on a clean surface. Brush it lightly with melted butter or olive oil. Place another sheet on top and brush it again. Repeat until you have 3-4 layers.

Add Filling:
- Place a spoonful of the spinach and cheese mixture at one end of the layered phyllo sheets. Fold the phyllo over the filling to form a triangle. Continue folding in a triangle shape until you reach the end of the phyllo.

Seal Edges:
- Brush the edges with more melted butter or olive oil to seal the triangle. Repeat the process with the remaining phyllo sheets and filling.

Bake:
- Place the prepared spanakopita triangles on a baking sheet. Bake in the preheated oven for 20-25 minutes or until golden brown and crispy.

Serve:
- Allow the spanakopita triangles to cool for a few minutes before serving. They can be enjoyed warm or at room temperature.

Tips:

- Cover the phyllo dough sheets with a damp towel while working to prevent them from drying out.
- Feel free to add a pinch of nutmeg or a squeeze of lemon juice to enhance the flavor of the filling.

Enjoy your homemade Greek Spanakopita Triangles!

Chicken Fried Steak with Country Gravy

Ingredients:

For Chicken Fried Steak:

- 4 cube steaks
- 1 cup all-purpose flour
- 1 teaspoon garlic powder
- 1 teaspoon onion powder
- 1 teaspoon paprika
- Salt and black pepper, to taste
- 2 large eggs
- 1/4 cup buttermilk
- Vegetable oil, for frying

For Country Gravy:

- 1/4 cup pan drippings (from frying the steak)
- 1/4 cup all-purpose flour
- 2 cups whole milk
- Salt and black pepper, to taste

Instructions:

Prepare Chicken Fried Steak:

Preheat Oven:
- Preheat the oven to 200°F (93°C) to keep the cooked steaks warm.

Set Up Breading Station:
- In one shallow dish, combine flour, garlic powder, onion powder, paprika, salt, and black pepper. In another dish, whisk together eggs and buttermilk.

Dredge Steaks:
- Dredge each cube steak in the seasoned flour mixture, coating both sides evenly. Shake off excess flour.

Dip in Egg Mixture:
- Dip the floured steak into the egg and buttermilk mixture, ensuring it's well coated.

Recoat in Flour Mixture:

- Place the steak back into the seasoned flour, pressing the flour onto the steak to adhere.

Fry Steaks:
- In a large skillet, heat vegetable oil over medium-high heat. Carefully place the breaded steaks into the hot oil. Fry each side until golden brown, about 4-5 minutes per side.

Drain and Keep Warm:
- Place the cooked steaks on a paper towel-lined plate to drain excess oil. Transfer them to a baking sheet in the preheated oven to keep warm.

Prepare Country Gravy:

Make Roux:
- In the same skillet with the pan drippings from frying the steaks, whisk in the flour over medium heat to make a roux.

Add Milk:
- Gradually add the milk to the roux, whisking constantly to avoid lumps. Cook until the gravy thickens, about 5-7 minutes.

Season:
- Season the gravy with salt and black pepper to taste. Continue to whisk until smooth.

Serve:

Plate Steaks:
- Place the chicken fried steaks on serving plates.

Pour Gravy:
- Pour the country gravy over the steaks, covering them generously.

Garnish:
- Garnish with chopped fresh parsley if desired.

Serve Warm:
- Serve the Chicken Fried Steak with Country Gravy immediately. Enjoy with mashed potatoes or your favorite sides.

Note:

- Adjust the seasoning in both the flour mixture and the gravy according to your taste preferences.

Enjoy your hearty Chicken Fried Steak with Country Gravy!

Fried Ice Cream Balls with Cinnamon Sugar

Ingredients:

For Fried Ice Cream Balls:

- 1 quart vanilla ice cream
- 2 cups cornflakes, crushed
- 1 cup shredded coconut
- 2 teaspoons ground cinnamon
- 1/2 cup honey
- Vegetable oil, for frying

For Cinnamon Sugar Coating:

- 1/2 cup granulated sugar
- 1 teaspoon ground cinnamon

Instructions:

Prepare Fried Ice Cream Balls:

   Scoop Ice Cream:
   - Using an ice cream scoop, form round balls of vanilla ice cream and place them on a parchment-lined tray. Freeze the ice cream balls until they are firm.

   Prepare Coating Mixture:
   - In a bowl, combine crushed cornflakes, shredded coconut, ground cinnamon, and honey. Mix well to form a thick, sticky coating mixture.

   Coat Ice Cream Balls:
   - Roll each frozen ice cream ball in the coating mixture, ensuring it is thoroughly coated. Place the coated balls back on the tray and freeze for at least 2 hours or until very firm.

   Double Coating (Optional):
   - For an extra crispy coating, you can repeat the coating process after the balls have frozen for the first time. Freeze again until very firm.

   Heat Oil:

- In a deep fryer or large, deep skillet, heat vegetable oil to 350°F (175°C).

Fry Ice Cream Balls:
- Carefully lower the coated ice cream balls into the hot oil using a slotted spoon or tongs. Fry for about 15-20 seconds until the coating is golden brown.

Drain and Serve:
- Remove the fried ice cream balls from the oil and place them on a paper towel-lined plate to drain excess oil.

Prepare Cinnamon Sugar Coating:

Combine Ingredients:
- In a shallow bowl, mix together granulated sugar and ground cinnamon to create the cinnamon sugar coating.

Coat Fried Ice Cream:
- Roll the hot fried ice cream balls in the cinnamon sugar mixture until they are well coated.

Serve Immediately:
- Serve the Fried Ice Cream Balls with Cinnamon Sugar immediately. They can be garnished with whipped cream, chocolate sauce, or caramel sauce if desired.

Enjoy your delightful Fried Ice Cream Balls with Cinnamon Sugar!

www.ingramcontent.com/pod-product-compliance
Lightning Source LLC
LaVergne TN
LVHW081607060526
838201LV00054B/2113